ALL
SORTS of
Clothes

For Fay Hillier. E.D.
For Eoin. H.R.

This paperback edition published in 2003
First published in Great Britain in 1999 by Zero To Ten Limited,
part of the Evans Publishing Group
2a Portman Mansions
Chiltern Street
London W1U 6NR

Copyright this edition © 2003 Zero to Ten Limited
Illustration copyright © 1999 Emma Dodd
Text copyright © 1999 Hannah Reidy

British Library Cataloguing in Publication Data
Reidy, Hannah
    All sorts of clothes
    1. Clothing and dress - Pictorial Works - Juvenile literature
    1. Title
    391

ISBN 1-84089-289-7

Printed in Hong Kong

ALL
SORTS of
Clothes

Written by Hannah Reidy
Illustrated by Emma Dodd

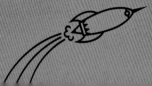

Becky loves her **checked** shirt, she wears it when she's working.

Cody's furry
collar keeps
him nice
and warm.

Owen loves his
buzzy bee suit.

Oscar
prefers his
BIG BOY
clothes.

Isaac doesn't like his itchy jumper.

He'd rather wear his soft sweatshirt.

Louise wears her **frilly** dress for parties.

Louie
wears his
frilly
shirt.

Liam's baseball cap looks **cool** with his Dad's new **sunglasses.**

Pippa has
lots of **pockets**
on her **stripy**
dungarees.

Toby's **teddy**
pyjamas are
soft and **warm**
and perfect for
dreaming.

What do you like to wear?